Praise For...
DON'T SELL THE CANDY STORE

"I wanted to tell you I read your entire book last night. I didn't think I was gonna be able to finish it [because] I was like 'oh I'm getting sleepy', but [...] honestly it was such a good read. I loved the parts where you're able to give examples because I love concrete examples and I learn that way, so that was [...] really helpful."

"I love that you said there is no magic formula, it's a lot of hard work. You are encouraging [a] decision. I think I like both, I need flexibility and balance."

"Clear who this is for, I like it. You are making people feel comfortable whichever camp they are in. I love the Candy Store Story."

"I read the book this past weekend and loved it."

"Congratulations Dennis. I read it, thought it was great and highly recommend it. Very readable with a lot of useful advice, especially to younger folks starting out in their careers."
Mark - Former Carvel Employee
Yale Law School Graduate

I wish Dennis good luck and God's favor in touching people's lives through this book. We've known each other for 70+ years and throughout this time as a compassionate and Godly person, always trying to help others. May his book bring joy and inspiration to others' lives.
Peter, Naples, FL

DENNIS MATZEL

DON'T SELL
THE CANDY STORE

ADVICE FROM 50+ YEARS OF BUSINESS

A STORY OF ENTREPRENEURSHIP

Don't Sell The Candy Store: A Story Of Entrepreneurship - Advice From 50+ Years Of Business

Copyright © 2025 by Dennis Matzel
Cover Image © 2025 by Dennis Matzel

This book is self-published in collaboration with: Rainy Day Self-Publishing LLC
    RainyDaySelfPublishing.com

All rights reserved. No part of this publication (or previous versions) may be reproduced, distributed, or transmitted in any form or by any means, including photocopying, recording, or other electronic or mechanical methods, without the prior written permission of the author, except in the case of brief quotations embodied in reviews and certain other noncommercial uses permitted by copyright law. To contact the author for permission requests, see below:
    Dennis Matzel
    dennismatzel.com or wisdomfinancialgrp.com or
    https://www.linkedin.com/in/dennis-matzel-86b2a11/
    dm@dennismatzel.com or info@wisdomfinancialgrp.com

Note: A portion of this book was once available online for free at the website named after this book. At this time, that option has been removed. This book contains updated material and is the only official version available.

The fonts used in this document are:
Garamond & Lucida Handwriting

For additional copies or bulk purchases, visit:
AUTHOR KDP SITE (Setup as soon as book is live)

Paperback ISBN: 979-8-9905699-1-1
Ebook ISBN: 979-8-9905699-2-8

Citations:
1. McRaven, W. H. (2017). *Make your bed: Little things that can change your life --and maybe the world.* Grand Central Publishing.
2. Helmstetter, S. (2017). *What to say when you talk to yourself.* Gallery Books.

Printed On Demand.

Dedication

I want to take a moment to thank a few individuals who helped make this book possible:

To my wife, life partner, and best friend. Thank you for putting up with me for 50+ years.

To my wonderful, beautiful family, my two daughters, and my grandkids, and my extended family and friends. I love you all and thank you for your support.

To Savannah Grace Newman, without you my book would still just be thoughts in my head. You helped bring the vision to paper. Thank you.

To Melissa Anne, you were able to take what Savannah started and bring it to the next stage. Thank you.

And to the team at Rainy Day Self-Publishing, you brought *Don't Sell The Candy Store* to the finish line. Thank you.

Contents

Introduction — i

One: Are You A Self-Starter? — 1
"Your actions speak so loudly, I cannot hear what you are saying."
- Ralph Waldo Emerson

Two: Knowing Your Why — 15
"To thine own self be true." - William Shakespeare,
Hamlet, Act I, Scene III

Three: What is Your Highest & Best Use? — 27
"Success comes when we identify our natural talents and
then work diligently to develop them into extraordinary
skills." - John C. Maxwell

Four: The Value Of Drilling — 35
"When all is said and done, more is said than done."
- Lou Holtz

Five: Build Your Support System — 41
"Ah, but I was so much older then, I'm younger than that now."
- Bob Dylan, My Back Pages

Six: Don't Be Deceived By Time — 49
"Experience is the hardest kind of teacher. It gives you the test first
and the lesson afterward." - Oscar Wilde

Seven: What Thoughts Are You Repeating? — 55
"If you don't like something, change it. If you can't
change it, change your attitude." - Maya Angelou

Eight: Should You Stay Or Should You Go? — 65
"Follow your passion - and if you don't know what it is, realize that
one reason for your existence on earth is to find it." - Oprah Winfrey

Nine: Don't Sell The Candy Store   73
"Never give in. Never give in. Never, never, never, never - in nothing, great or small, large or petty - never give in, except to convictions of honor and good sense" - Winston Churchill

Photos   79
Prompts   89
About The Author   97
Interested In Mentorship   97

Introduction

Are you feeling stuck in life? Not feeling satisfied with your position in this world? Maybe you dread starting your day. You find yourself lying in bed staring at the clock as your alarm goes off, wanting to sleep in and never return to work again.

Maybe you find yourself constantly on autopilot, feeling so unfulfilled with the tasks that you do on a weekly and monthly basis that it barely feels like living at all. It feels like your soul is being sucked right out of you, and all joy is gone. But it used to be there, right? The joy. The feelings of fulfillment. So, what changed?

How can you create a more fulfilling life? One that affects not just yourself, but the community that surrounds you as well.

My guess is that you know what needs to change, or at least an inkling. I mean, these are some reasons why people read self-help books anyway, *right*?

While I may not know you personally, I have a feeling that you came to the right place to start getting yourself out of whatever rut you found yourself stuck in. Whether it's to inspire you or help you realize you might actually have it pretty good, you simply need a little shift in perspective.

Now you might wonder, "*Who the heck is this guy?*" and "*Why should I read his book?*" Both are valid questions. The short answer: I'm simply a man leaving behind a little piece of my story, hoping to impact two people:

The **first person** is someone I can encourage to take the plunge and jump into entrepreneurship. I'll be the nudge needed to get off the nine-to-five track and start pursuing what they truly feel called to go after. I'll provide them with key life lessons from my 50+ years of business to help them see that it can be achievable and sustainable for them, too.

For this person, my book will inspire, motivate, and help them change their mindset around building the business they need to achieve the success and the lifestyle they dream of.

The **second person** is the one I want to discourage from getting into entrepreneurship. "But Dennis, why would you ever want to discourage someone from something you've spent your whole life doing?" I realize that this might sound like a bad thing at first, but I hope that by discouraging this person, I can save them from a lot of headaches, grief, and misery. Possibly even helping them avoid spending a lot of money, maybe even a life savings.

After reading this book, they may realize that they are content with their corporate job, and perhaps just need a shift in perspective around how it provides for the lifestyle they enjoy. Knowing I've done this for either person will mean this book was a success.

The truth is that entrepreneurship isn't for the faint of heart. But it is worthwhile!

This book is my way of highlighting what 50 years of being in business looks like, not shying away from the ups, the downs, and everything in between that led me to where I am today. Each chapter focuses on key aspects of both personal and business life, as they often go hand in hand and affect one another over time.

Later, I will explain what I mean by saying, "*don't sell the candy store,*" as my title states. A story I have included just before the first chapter for those that need a quick overview now.

However, my recommendation would be to read this book in its entirety. Rather than skipping and assuming the answer, get to know my story and what led me to almost sell the candy store in my own life. In some ways, I kind of did, but you'll learn more about that later.

My Backstory

I grew up in New York City in the late 1950s when kids played outside every day. I've always been a self-starter. In fact, I started working as a newspaper boy at the age of 14.

By 16, I was working at a Carvel Ice Cream Franchise down the block from my school. Soon after high school, I served in the Vietnam War and then owned a Carvel Ice Cream Franchise shortly after my service.

I have had my hands in many different businesses over my life, spending the last 50+ years being self-employed. It has provided me with the lifestyle I have always wanted even if at times it was a bumpy road. I made it through every time.

Throughout this book's chapters, you'll learn from my many mistakes over the years and ways to avoid making them in your own life and business. Whether you decide that entrepreneurship is the right move for you or that sticking to a corporate job is what you need most, I'm here to support you in reigniting joy in your life both personally and professionally.

If I've piqued your curiosity, I encourage you to continue reading.

The Candy Store

There was a young man who moved to New York from another country with his family. He needed some way to make a living to provide for his family, so he opened a candy store. You know, a kiosk, aka, "Candy Store", you find on the streets in major cities. It was stocked with newspapers, candy, etc.

He risked everything to start this, but he had the need and desire to take care of his loved ones. So, he worked hard every day, he opened his Candy Store, took care of his customers, and serviced them well.

Because of his hard work, he became very successful. He became so successful that he had a surplus income. After thinking about it, he decided that he would buy into real estate with the extra money. But he continued to work hard at the Candy Store while he was accumulating the real estate.

He had so many different revenue streams that he was able to take care of his family far more than he could have ever imagined before his move from his home country.

Despite how successful he was, he never sold the Candy Store. He figured if all went south, and he lost all the real estate, he knew he could always go back to running the Candy Store and provide for his family. And that's what he did.

In this book, I'll explain how this story has shaped me and why you shouldn't *sell the Candy Store* in your own life. Now, as far as what that means, we'll get to that later. Even if the Candy Store in your own life isn't a physical thing, it is still a foundation that you should never get rid of.

Let's get to it.

CHAPTER ONE

Are You A Self-Starter?

> *"Your actions speak so loudly, I cannot hear what you are saying."*
> **Ralph Waldo Emerson**

Being a self-starter is an absolute necessity when it comes to business success. If you can't push yourself to get things done, no one else is going to. It's not like other working environments where someone is telling you what to do, where to be, and when to be there. Every task within a business is on you. You're in charge of everything.

For some, this might sound exciting. For others, this could be a challenge. However, this is essential if you truly aspire to become a successful business owner. Being a self-starter isn't always easy. There will be tough days when you simply *don't want to.*

You might be feeling incredibly sick, mental health struggles may come up, or you might lack motivation. Nevertheless, at times like these, you must do it unmotivated, pushing forward no matter what your fears and feelings but more about this later.

Getting ourselves to do things we don't want to do is one of the biggest challenges for everything in life. How do you get yourself past the challenge of not wanting to?

My opinion is that your why has to be big enough. Being a self-starter goes hand in hand with having a big enough why, something we'll dive deeper into the next chapter.

Let me tell you a story I heard, oh I don't know... 40 years ago. It may not be true, but the meaning is what matters most:

It was a warm, sunny day in the Old West. When the weather was this nice, the women would go out with their babies wrapped in blankets to enjoy the sun.

Well, one day, when the babies were out, a large bird came down thinking one of them was prey, grabbed the baby with its talons, and flew to the top of the mountain. Everyone was going nuts. The mother, of course, was going crazy.

I mean, imagine if it was your baby. So, the men got together and were like, "Okay... here's what we're going to do." These men organized how they were going to get this baby back. They were warriors and hunters, after all. Back then women didn't really do that kind of stuff.

The men are up on this mountain, working towards the top. But they get to a certain point, a flat surface, and don't know how to get past it. So, they decide, "Let's regroup and figure out how to overcome this obstacle." Once they get back down to huddle, they look up and see that the mom is at the top ledge of the mountain, grabbing the baby.

All the men are confused, asking the woman, "What the heck, how did you figure it out?" And the woman's response was, "That wasn't your baby."

When we have challenges to overcome, we have to function as business owners. If we aren't finding a way to get into the self-starter mentality, we won't get crucial tasks done that are needed to succeed.

Like the woman in this story, her why for pushing past the obstacles of the flat surface was saving her baby. There was no other choice but to achieve success. Though strong and capable, the men didn't have the why big enough to push forward as quickly as the mother.

I'll give another example of self-starting from my personal life. In my early 20s, my family and I put together the money needed to buy a Carvel Franchise. While serving in Vietnam and Germany, I managed to have $10,000 saved, my father cashed in his pension, and we borrowed some money from family. While I didn't have the money on my own, we found a way to make it happen.

After purchasing the store, I could have easily slumped around avoiding getting tasks completed, but my family and I invested too much money not to make things happen.

Where did I get the energy from?
I didn't. I simply knew it had to be done.

Being a self-starter is two percent motivation and ninety-eight percent perspiration. How can you build up the momentum to accomplish what needs to be done? Step out of your comfort zone and get to it.

So many people think there's this magic formula. They spend more time looking for it than getting stuff done.

Here's a little secret...
there is no magic formula.

It's a lot of hard work. It's learning to just do it because your why is big enough. You have to choose to commit to yourself and others. Whether those others are a family you want to provide a specific lifestyle for, clients and customers you want to support positive relations with, or both.

Keep your long-term goals in mind. Let go of the instant gratification mentality and figure out what it takes to keep pushing forward. How will you get up every day and do the tasks you know need to be done to reach your goals?

I don't know how true either of these stories are, but I can remember reading a story about how Mike Tyson's push had always been his opponents. If they were getting up at 4:00 am, he would get up at 2:00 am.

The other story was about when Michael Jordan didn't make the basketball team. His mom didn't sugarcoat things to make him feel better. She made her son get back to the gym and try harder.

They were both given a reason to keep going and look at what they both have done because of it!

If you are looking for a magic answer, you better stick to fairy tales. Because here in the real world, you gotta dig down deep. You have to create the magic here. And the magic ingredients are hard work and grit.

When things are hard and motivation is at an all-time low, things like knowing your why come into play. Keeping in mind the end goal helps you remember that it is worth the sacrifice of "*not wanting to do it*." But what do I know, I'm just a guy that's been doing this for 50+ years, right?

Can you take the initiative?

Can you see a need and act on it without someone telling you to do so? Because this is another crucial piece of the self-starter aspect of running a business. Entrepreneurs are regularly looking for opportunities. We are proactive.

Rather than sitting around and hoping for the right opportunity to land on our doorstep, we are creating them.

Whether you're an entrepreneur, interested in entrepreneurship, or working in the corporate field, you've likely experienced applying for a job at least once in your life.

A corporation isn't going to knock on your door and ask you to work for them. You have to submit the application yourself - at least 99% of the time. The same goes for creating opportunities in your life.

If you're still struggling with getting started and keeping the momentum going, consider doing a self-examination. Be realistic when doing this. And no, I don't mean a physical examination.

I mean a mental and practical examination of your talents, strengths, and weaknesses in comparison to what you're trying to accomplish.

I'll give an example from my own experience. At this point in my life, I already had my Carvel Franchise store paid off and was ready for another career venture.

I was fortunate enough to be with my wife during the delivery of our first daughter. After experiencing my wife's delivery, I remember physically shaking because I hadn't seen something this incredible in my life. I thought, "*There's my calling*," and thought about going to medical school.

But I didn't think about the realism of pursuing this career path. What was the likelihood of me going back to school? I hadn't taken any science classes such as organic chemistry, physics, etc. Not only would I need to take a whole bunch of classes, but I would have to get pretty good grades to even apply to medical school. At that time, I didn't have the intellect or inclination to pursue this avenue.

I had to have an honest talk with myself and accept that it was realistically never going to happen. I struggled enough to even study for finals. Medical school would be a full-time job of learning all the material. It just wasn't practical. My why wouldn't have been strong enough to be a self-starter in medical school.

A similar self-examination came to me while in aviation school, a story I will share more in chapter eight about deciding whether to stay or go. While in the program, I had to ask myself why I wasn't all in with it. It took an honest reflection on if I was simply making excuses, or if it was simply a career path that didn't align with me.

Entrepreneurship, on the other hand, always ignited a drive. I craved flexibility. But with that flexibility has come things like sometimes being up until ten or eleven at night reviewing projects for business clients. Something that not everyone will have a big enough why to pursue and keep momentum with.

Some may decide that they prefer the structure of a nine-to-five schedule with weekends off, though, and that's perfectly okay. Others might just need to create a similar structure with their own business.

There is an unofficial motto that many postal service employees carry with them. The words are engraved in front of the James A. Farley Post Office in NYC and are as follows:

"Neither snow nor rain nor heat nor gloom of night stays these couriers from the swift completion of their appointed rounds."

That is the same motto I adopted at 14 years old, working a paper route for my very first job. My first taste of being a self-starter.

I delivered papers every day regardless of the snow, rain, heat, etc. It started as a way for me to buy the things I wanted, but a passion for honoring my commitment to people kept me motivated during the most challenging days.

To give you an idea of my schedule, I had 92 to 98 papers to deliver seven days a week. After school, I used to go to the station to pick up the papers, around two or three in the afternoon, and the summertime was no different. All of us paperboys would have to load the papers up in our basket in front of our bikes, and then we delivered the papers that day.

At first, it felt overwhelming trying to remember which area I was working, but after a while, I had the route memorized to the point where I could just zip through the four blocks and another two blocks to get all of my papers delivered in a timely manner.

I could have easily allowed that challenge to keep me from continuing the newspaper route. Instead, I gave myself the time to grow and build momentum with the tasks I needed to accomplish each week.

In the summertime, many of the kids would dump their papers in the trash and head to the beach. Where we lived in New York, we were maybe half an hour from the beach by train, so it was incredibly tempting to follow suit. At the same time, I didn't understand.

The other paperboys had customers expecting them to deliver papers, and those customers tipped well for good service. The better job you did, the better you got tipped.

I knew there would be temporary joy from skipping my delivery route and having fun with the other kids my age, but there would have also been a guilt of knowing it wasn't the right thing to do. This is something that ties into self-discipline and is necessary to be successfully self-employed.

Around the holidays, like Christmas time, if you did a good job, customers would tip you a few dollars, which was incredible money considering that back then, ten cents was an okay tip. When we did an exceptional job, we were rewarded. It was as simple as that.

All that being said, I would show up rain or shine to deliver those papers because I knew it paid off.

I would still question momentarily what I was doing, though, why I was putting so much effort into this paper route when others weren't taking it nearly as seriously.

But I had to remember that while most kids my age were only focused on themselves and short-term wins, I was focused on how my actions affected others and the long-term benefits of my actions - another necessity if you're going to maintain solid customer relations in business.

The kids who threw away the papers still got paid by the week. If, on the off chance, someone called to complain, they would just make up an excuse that they missed the house. But did they get that Christmas tip from their customers? Did they truly understand hard work? Or learn integrity? I think not. I had to learn to deny myself to get the job done. Knowing the long-term results would be so much more worthwhile.

I can still remember delivering in the wintertime. The wind was so strong, and the temperature was probably down to the single digits or lower. Mind you, I'm not driving. I'm pedaling my bike against these super strong winds; it was so cold, and I was freezing.

It was normal for me to get up around five in the morning, maybe six at the very latest, every Sunday to get paper deliveries done early. People would get up, and they wanted to read the newspaper with their morning coffee and breakfast. So, you couldn't deliver something around 10:00 am. You had to have all the papers done by seven or eight on Sunday mornings.

Sundays were also a big day because these papers were ten times as big as they were during the weekdays. They were gigantic, not at all like they are today. So, it was a lot of work to pedal against the wind and get these papers delivered in a timely fashion against the freezing cold during the winter, but I still made it happen - rain, shine, or even through the awful winter storms.

Not everyone is a self-starter.

I share my newspaper route story as an example of what a self-starter looks, thinks, and acts like even at a young age compared to those who aren't, like some of the other paper boys who simply wanted to play. It was evident who took the initiative and cared about the customer experience out of our group.

To be successful in business, you must be willing to push yourself even on the hard days. I could have easily chosen not to deliver papers on those miserable days, but I kept the bigger picture in mind.

It was keeping that why in mind that made the hard days worth it. Whether it was getting money for the things I wanted or seeing satisfied customers, I chose to show up every day, seven days a week.

Not many kids could say they were self-sufficient at 14, but I began to take pride in being able to buy all the things I wanted without having to beg my parents, or even get their permission, to do so. If I wanted a new bike, I was able to buy one. During the holidays, I was even able to afford presents to give to my family.

I could have continued grumbling and bothering my parents. I probably would have received a nice shirt or two, so my mom would get me off her back, but I would have been back to bugging her when those went out of style.

Instead, I gained this newfound independence through working that allowed me to have the money I wanted and the freedom to spend it where I chose to do so - a lesson I have since carried on throughout the years.

Fast forward to high school, and I could be found working 20 hours per week at a Carvel Ice Cream Franchise down the block from school. I was earning $0.90 an hour, the minimum wage at the time, while in school, then 40 hours or more per week over the summer.

Much like my experience with the paper route, it was up to my own self-determination to make the profits I wanted to see for the lifestyle I wanted to live.

Even though I didn't need much at the age of 16, I still worked hard. I didn't complain about the tasks I was given, because I knew the rewards that came from grit while on the newspaper route.

Getting what you want is possible, but it won't come without hard work. However, hard work doesn't mean it can't be enjoyable work.

You have to be a self-starter if you want to reach success as an entrepreneur. Realizing you will have to work to achieve your dreams is essential. There is so much talk out there about "passive income," but the truth is that it all requires some level of consistent work. It's just a matter of what level of work doesn't feel soul-draining for you.

When you're on your own, you won't have a boss nagging at your shoulder to "get to work." It is all on you to put in the effort. Choose a path that genuinely feels fulfilling to you.

Not having a boss nagging me was one of the biggest reasons I chose to become an entrepreneur to begin with. After serving in the Army during Vietnam, I knew I was too free-spirited to be taking orders from someone else especially when that someone doesn't seem to have the same values as me.

Let me ask you this: *Are your dreams worth the grit needed to achieve them, or will you decide that it's easier to simply be told what to do and where to be? Neither is wrong or right, but it is a decision you have to make, knowing whether to pursue a career path or not.*

Now as I mentioned in the introduction, I'm here for two people. The one that wants to pursue entrepreneurship but needs a little reminding of the sacrifices, and the other that needs a reminder that it's okay to work a nine-to-five job. My ultimate goal is to see you fulfilled.

My father worked for the same company for 43 years outside his short time serving in World War II. He watched three generations of this family-owned company come and go after becoming millionaires.

A friend of his was in business and I would regularly hear my father have conversations about how this friend "had it made" financially, but he still chose to keep his corporate position.

He loved what he did and knew that it provided for his family the way he wanted to provide. Even if it meant making a fraction of the money the generational family owners left with, or never having it made the way his friend seemed to have it. My father was content enough to stay.

At one point he made a partial attempt at starting a business, but after the first investor said no, my dad never tried again. Sure, he could have kept trying, but he still appreciated what his company did for him and how he was able to provide for his family. So, he stayed with that company until retirement.

His why for staying with the company was stronger than his why for continuing to pursue a business goal.

My father's career path gave me proof that a "normal" job could be an excellent choice for some, but I knew it wasn't for me. It might be for you, though. Know that the decision is yours whether you choose to pursue a career up the corporate ladder or the entrepreneurial route. Neither is better or worse. It's your life to live however you deem fit.

"*What if I'm not a self-starter?*" There are things you can start practicing and implementing into your daily life to build the habit it takes to become one.

You can start with good habits such as waking up and making your bed[1]. Doing something as mundane as making a bed with its limited rewards can trickle into doing other tasks throughout your day with similar seemingly little rewards in the here and now, but with longer-term benefits.

Completing mundane tasks reminds us that not everything will bring us instant gratification, but they can provide longer-term rewards.

The truth is that seeing a put-together bed at the end of the day compared to a pile of messy sheets truly can positively affect you and help with momentum. Much like putting dirty dishes away immediately rather than waiting for dishes to pile up can have long-term rewards.

Creating routines makes it much easier to combat negative thinking and procrastination. Like when I delivered those Sunday papers. I knew that once I was done with the last delivery, I could use the rest of the day for myself. It's similar to working within a nine-to-five job, except you're creating the schedule for yourself with the tasks you accomplish throughout the week and month.

You can start small. In fact, starting small is essential for long-term habits to stick. Start with a morning or bedtime routine. This helps you become more organized and disciplined within your personal life and can begin to trickle into your business efforts as well. You can even create a reward system for following your routines.

You have to find what your motivation is. Especially on those hard days or as you're beginning to implement these new tools you may find you will lack the success you are truly looking for. We'll discuss this in more detail in the next chapter.

If you do find that you're constantly procrastinating, take a moment and go back to the self-examination.

Why could you be procrastinating on the tasks you know are needed to reach the goals you say you want to accomplish? It might simply be laziness, a lack of structure, or not getting that instant gratification feel-good experience.

It could also be a sign of something just not aligning. Look at the self-examination of what you're working towards, your strengths and weaknesses, and be realistic. Maybe it's time to look into different areas of work where you feel more inspired to act and start to achieve your goals. Your why for this current area just might not be big enough to work past the obstacles it takes to achieve success.

A lot of people say they want to get into business, but many never take the first step. And I'm not even talking big steps. Forget about the big steps. I've coached several different people over the years that talk the talk about how great the idea is of owning a business, but they never take the tiny steps forward.

Over the last few decades, I've given a list of steps to different people in my life who have come to me for advice about what to do and where to begin. Do you know how many of them did something about it when we caught back up weeks or months later? Almost none of them.

Why? Because they aren't a self-starter. Their reason for starting the business isn't good enough to sacrifice the free time they have to accomplish even the baby steps. It's okay if you're not a self-starter, but you must figure out what will help you stay accountable to completing tasks if you truly want to succeed.

Talk is cheap. You could talk for hours over the course of years about how you're going to start up this great business idea one day, but the truth is that many times that excuse will keep you stuck.

It's up to you to look at your current lifestyle and decide what sacrifices or adjustments are needed. Rather than watching another episode on TV, or sleeping in the extra hour, look at ways to make the time needed for the baby steps towards your goals in current time. Because too soon, "generally" never actually arrives. It just delays your success.

The truth is that many people are so comfortable with their

current jobs that they aren't willing to sacrifice that comfort for the unknown. I wanted the opposite.

It was largely because I had more confidence in my own abilities than in Corporate America. The last job I held was in the military and that was enough for me. Not having people telling me what to do or where to be, and everything being on their terms was huge.

Something to keep in mind when it comes to being a self-starter and getting tasks done is the reminder that some people work better when told what to do. Maybe you are a good self-starter, you just need the added push for deadlines. It's almost like being back in school.

Many of us wait until the last few days before studying or getting tasks accomplished because we do better with the added pressure. We have no choice but to buckle down and get it done, otherwise we'll fail. Working towards business goals is a similar process.

Chapter Two

Knowing Your Why

> *"To thine own self be true."*
> **William Shakespeare**
> **Hamlet, Act I, Scene III**

What is driving you to enter entrepreneurship? Your answer will likely look different from others, and that's okay. It's also okay for your answer to change over the years as your life circumstances change. Knowing your why can help shape the direction you go in your business journey and the adjustments you make along the way.

Taking the first step towards realizing what I wanted and how I could achieve it was a huge milestone in my childhood. Though it started with something seemingly small, such as having extra change in my pocket to spend money on the things I enjoyed, it still made my hours of newspaper deliveries in not-so-ideal weather beyond worth it.

Fast forward to early adulthood, and my why shifted. I was no longer a little kid. I had a future family I knew I'd want to support one day and a particular lifestyle I wanted to provide for them when the time came.

You see, before serving in the military, the owner of a local Carvel Ice Cream franchise I worked at throughout high school took me under his wing and gave me my first real taste of what business success could look like. I will never forget it.

He had a beautiful home in Long Island with a wife, a family, and a swimming pool. My boss was able to provide this incredible lifestyle with amazing vacations for himself and his family. I remember being amazed that all of this came from selling ice cream.

This experience opened my eyes to entrepreneurship and made me truly start thinking about it more seriously. Seeing the lifestyle my boss created in his own life inspired me to continue working hard in mine. I had discovered a new why. But knowing your why doesn't mean business will be easy or that things will go your way.

In many ways, it didn't go smoothly for me.

Back in 1968, military registration was a requirement for all males. I had just graduated high school in '67 and got placed into the draft system by 19 years of age. I had a very high draft number, which meant I was very likely to get drafted and not have a clue where I would end up in the Vietnam War

Since I was already mentally prepared to end up in Vietnam, I sat wondering what I could do to end up in the base camp, or who knows what job they would have assigned to me.

I spoke to an Army recruiter about options right away. We discussed school options for different military jobs I could do, but I wasn't ready to commit to the idea yet.

A few weeks later, I got the induction letter for service in the military, gave the recruiter a call, and enlisted into the military rather than getting drafted so I could be guaranteed a school date for a job of my choice, not the Army's.

It worked out exactly as I hoped it would. After enlisting in the Army, I spent the next eight months between basic training and specialty training for aviation.

Then I was off to the Vietnam War. This is a perfect example of taking initiative in your life. Sure, I applied it in the previous chapter to the importance of self-employment, but it can apply to any career path.

You are capable of navigating your career's direction. It is your life, after all. Right?

If I was able to have some control over my military experience, you're capable of making moves in the direction that matches your career goals, too.

Even though I was able to choose my path within the Army, it didn't come without its share of struggles. I remember my first moments arriving in Vietnam like it was yesterday. After stopping in Alaska, then Japan, Thailand, and finally Vietnam, I made it to the airfield around the Saigon area. I hadn't showered in three to four days. I felt so clammy. It was scorching hot. I remember thinking, "*I have to take a shower."*

Mind you, I didn't have a towel or clean clothes. All I had were the dirty, sweaty military fatigues that I currently had on. But I needed a refresh, so I hopped in the shower anyway. As I was showering, I saw this Vietnamese lady cleaning the showers and I remember thinking, "*This is kind of odd!*"

After showering, I dried off with the same dirty clothes I was wearing, putting the dirty pants, socks, shirt, and everything back on. That's when it hit me. The realization that I'm in a foreign country, one where foreign women are cleaning showers while I'm showering.

That realization brought with it the reminder that I was in a combat zone and there were people who wanted to kill me. I was in a different world now and would be stuck here for 12 months.

I remember telling myself, "*Look, there's only two ways out of here. You can go AWOL to France or Canada, or you can go out in a pine box. Those are the only ways you're getting out of here early.*" But I knew I wouldn't do the first. My dad was in World War II and was so proud of my service.

I started freaking out. Paranoia set in. I had never been in a position where I couldn't leave. But then I got back to my senses. I told myself, "*You have a choice to make, young man. You're going to make the best of this, or you're going to fall apart.*" I chose then and there that I was going to make the best of this, with positive thinking in my head.

Vietnam wasn't a cakewalk just because I was on the airfield. We would have nights where we'd get rocketed and mortared. So many nights we would go in these bunkers - this hole in the ground with sandbags covering it, supposedly there to protect us.

But it was honestly kind of a joke because if a rocket hit us there, we would die anyway. More people got hurt by stubbing a toe or getting bit by a venomous creature just trying to get to the bunker in time.

So, after a while, we decided, "*to heck with it,*" and would crawl under the bed rack every time we'd get attacked rather than run to the bunker and risk other injuries.

I remember praying any time a rocket or mortar would head

toward our airfield. As the crackling sounds moved closer, all we really could do was pray. Nothing else could be done at that point, so I'd pray something like, "*Dear God, please don't let this rocket hit us,*" and slowly try to get back to bed afterward.

After what felt like an eternity, I finally left the Vietnam War and ended up stationed in Germany for my last year of service. With the money I saved from my year in Vietnam, I was even able to buy a new Volkswagen (aka a Bug). After a high-stress year, it felt good to have something nice to show for it, without the fear of getting rocketed throughout the night.

You see, even though I had my why in mind, life still brought me through a few rough turns and career path redirections. All choices that were ultimately up to me.

After serving my three years in the military, I was honorably discharged and left with the decision as to what direction to head in at that point in my life. Thankfully, I saved a decent amount of money while in the military. There wasn't much to spend on while in Vietnam or Germany. Something that helped me out a lot once I decided I didn't want to stay in aviation school (something you'll learn more about in Chapter Eight) because it allowed me time to realign.

Fresh from the military and a recent aviation school dropout, I no longer knew what I was doing with my life. What I did know was that I had Veterans Benefits that I could apply towards going to college.

Unfortunately, I didn't realize that high school was for learning. I just thought it was for having fun and meeting people.

When it came time for me to enroll in a community college, I had to take almost an entire year of no-credit classes to learn how to read, write, and create better study habits because my high school grades were terrible.

But something unusual happened. Once I got involved in taking classes, I started to realize that I loved learning. At this point, I was maybe 22 or 23. I was like a sponge, absorbing everything I could get my hands on.

All I wanted to do was take classes I thought were enjoyable without worrying about a degree, and I did. I ended up taking all kinds of cool classes like philosophy, seventeenth-century literature, poetry, you name it.

College helped me find a second love for something I didn't even know I was really interested in. Of course, the tests and papers weren't enjoyable, but the learning was. In many ways, college also helped reignite a spark I needed to start pursuing new ventures in life.

The vision I had from that Carvel owner stuck with me though. His lifestyle was still a huge goal of mine. After a few conversations with my parents, we put together the money needed for me to become an official owner of a Carvel Ice Cream Franchise at the age of 23. Cashing in retirement, savings, scraping up enough money to put in for the down payment.

And let me tell you, even with the vision in mind of the Carvel owner I worked for as a high school kid, it wasn't at all what I pictured it would be like, at least at the start. I wasn't just a kid who worked there a few hours a week. I owned one.

Everything was now on my shoulders to keep it successful. My family gave every bit to help support this path of mine. I couldn't let them down. I had no other choice but to be successful. For them, for me.

My first year in business was probably the most difficult one. From time to time, my father would come to help me, but for the most part, it was all on me. I got up every day and worked from around nine in the morning until midnight, fifteen to eighteen-hour days, seven days a week. It was long, hard hours of work.

I didn't have a day off for a whole year. Not even the holidays. I might as well have lived inside that Carvel because I didn't even go out to eat.

One of my worst days was when I had a bad case of the flu. It was a Sunday morning, and I had to go to work because I had no one else to open the store. I was fresh into the franchise. I didn't have any other management type employees to open or close my store yet.

I took a shower, got dressed, and drove forty-five minutes into Brooklyn to work a twelve-hour shift. And let me tell you, when I got home, I almost didn't even make it into the bed. I was so beat.

Not just physically exhausted but emotionally too. It had me questioning if this was what I really wanted. To have such challenging days like this, and for what?

Another event that had me heavily questioning my choice to own a Carvel franchise was one summer night during my first year. There was a disco near my house in Queens. My Carvel was in Brooklyn, so it was about a twenty or thirty-minute drive home.

Well, I was driving home one night after working eighteen hours. I was dirty, sweaty, and smelled like an ice cream shop. My whites were completely covered with ice cream and chocolate syrup. You name the topping, and it was likely on them.

Anyway, it was around midnight, and I heard a lot of noise coming from a disco near my home. If you don't know, the disco is a club where we could go dancing, partying, etc. I decided to park to the side of the building and was immediately taken over by emotions, tears streaming down my face.

There I was, in my early 20s, working my tail off, completely exhausted, and these other kids my age were out having the time of their lives. It felt defeating. I had to ask myself if it was worth it. All the sacrifices I was making to have the things these other kids didn't have at my age.

It brought me back to an expression I would hear from a Carvel customer all the time, "*you have to walk while you're young so you can ride while you're old.*"

I also remembered the words my attorney shared with me when buying my Carvel location. He has said, "*You know you're gonna have tough times, but it will be worth it. You have an opportunity that a lot of people don't have...*" I learned that to be very true.

And you know what? It did get easier.

After the first year, I was finally able to start taking time off, and eventually, it gave me and my family the lifestyle I was looking for. I'm talking about trips to places like Acapulco, Mexico, Curacao, Aruba, Florida, etc. I had a beautiful home in Long Island, new cars, you name it.

But quite frankly, it was all ego-driven. I went from not having a lot and working myself to the bone to having a surplus of both time and money.

I mean, I didn't have to go on a vacation every month at the age of 23. But there I was talking with guys in their sixties and seventies who had worked their whole lives to finally go on a trip that I did once a month. I was even buying investment property in Florida to increase our net worth.

Your why doesn't always have to be about the lifestyle you want to live. For some, your reason for entrepreneurship might be more focused on the change you wish to bring to this world.

Rather than being motivated by houses, cars, and vacations, maybe your why is impact-driven on a larger scale. You could have a vision or goal to help non-profit organizations shape the lives of hundreds or thousands of individuals.

Keep your goal in mind.

Think about the problem your future customers or clients might be struggling with and how showing up for your business each day can help improve their lives.

Once you've narrowed down your why, it's important to keep it in the front of your mind. Some ways of doing this include: creating a vision board, leaving Post-It notes at your workstation, or even repeating your why out loud, in your head, or writing in a journal regularly. Whatever helps keep you pushing forward and remembering your why is what you should focus on.

Understanding your why will also help you align with the business plan needed for the lifestyle you want to live and the impact you want to have within this world. Aligning your personal values with your business values will be largely important.

These values can include the time you have to spend with loved ones, going out to a disco, work-life boundaries, and so forth.

What does your dream life look like? What type of home are you living in? What activities are you doing throughout the month? What does your daily routine look like? How do you show up each day? Take a moment to visualize all of this as if you already have it.

Now, slowly start working backward with how your knowledge and skill sets can provide you with the lifestyle you want. If you're not exactly sure what you have to offer, we'll dive into that in the next chapter about discovering your highest and best use when it comes to business.

Keep in mind that although I keep saying business, this can be applied to any career path. Does your current job help you with your why? If it doesn't, let's get you there.

Let me share some examples from people I've mentored over the years.

Example one: *A young lady within the medical field was torn between continuing to work abroad. After graduating from college, she started serving in a hospital and felt so incredibly fulfilled within this field that she didn't really want to come back and work within the United States. She loved who she served, and the impact she had on the people living within this country, as a medical professional.*

The problem was that her why was starting to shift. Even being fulfilled in this career path, she knew that getting married and having a family was next on her list.

Her dilemma was whether she should continue on this career path in a third-world country, or move back to her home state in hopes of meeting someone she could start a family with.

We held a conversation about what to do while she was visiting. After having a heart-to-heart, she decided to continue pursuing this career path she was so passionate about, trusting that she would meet someone when the time was right.

She ended up meeting someone overseas at the same hospital she was passionate about serving and fulfilled with working at. They ended up getting married and now have a family together.

This lady could have let go of her greatest passion only to find a new hospital back home that she wasn't nearly as passionate about. Instead, she stayed focused on her why to serve in this third-world country, while keeping her longer-term goals in mind. She trusted that showing up authentically, keeping in mind her why, would pay off.

Example two: *Many kids think that they will become the next pro ball player in whatever sport they're involved in. Not nearly as many of them are willing to put in the effort to make it a reality. Can you guess the reason for this? Their why isn't big enough.*

Sure, the idea of making it big sounds good in theory but applying the tasks needed to actually make it happen isn't nearly as appealing.

Once practice is over, most players don't care to continue practicing and improving their skill sets. The difference between a pro ball player and someone who just thinks it sounds good is effort. There's never a true off-season if you're going the professional route.

The season might be over for the school year. Winter might even prevent outdoor practices. But neither of these things should keep someone passionate about becoming a professional athlete from showing up each day. It's what is done outside of the spotlight that matters.

Your why needs to be strong enough to overcome different challenges, because there are going to be a lot of challenges that come up in businesses. The issue is that a lot of people want a quick fix.

Too many people will start a business and feel like a hotshot. Maybe they bought a sign or business cards to hand out. But buying those types of things doesn't mean anything unless you go and use them.

It's like the regular complaints of, "I hate my job. I can't stand this" but never doing anything to change it.

You've actually got to do something to see success. Work past the challenges and excuses. Otherwise, you won't be doing much of anything except going nowhere fast.

Some challenges that can come up include complacency. Many of the people I've mentored have found themselves too comfortable with where they're at. Sure, they have big dreams, but complacency, nervousness, or too small of a why keeps them stuck.

__Here's another example:__ Someone is working within the medical field. They've been in this position for probably about ten years now. We've talked several times now, and they always say how they're going to go back to school one of these days.

By going back to school for two years they could increase their hourly wage by nearly double. Can you imagine making double your current income simply by going to school for two years?

But this person hasn't done it. They like the idea of making more money, but their why isn't big enough to sacrifice and work through the tasks needed to reach the next level.

Many talk about going into business but aren't going to do it because their why isn't big enough to overcome obstacles. "*Someday...*" It's not going to happen.

The excuse is often, "I'm not going to give all that up." So, they will have a boss with weekends off rather than tackling the myriad of obstacles which might come up 24/7 in the life of an entrepreneur.

You can still balance a job and work on the business. The issue is that it requires you to get off work and skip the streaming platforms or video games. If your why isn't big enough to sacrifice some free time for future you, you won't make it.

One of the hardest parts is the transformation of working full time while working towards another goal. It requires a huge why, conviction, and getting out of your comfort zone. It also generally doesn't hit instant satisfaction, which causes us to stop pursuing and completing tasks. Forgetting about, or totally lacking, the five- to ten-year vision.

A quick reminder: this sacrifice isn't going to last forever.

It won't always be necessary to work all these hours, but it comes with letting go of instant wins at the start. It's going to be hard for a little bit, but it'll be worth it for the vacations and time off. There is a light at the end of the tunnel. I know because I've done it and made it.

One of my biggest whys for pushing through was not having a boss I had to request time off with. I loved knowing that how much or how little I worked each week, or month was entirely on me.

But I also know sacrifice. There was one point in my life when I was working 10 to 12 hours a day on Carvel, then taking the limited free time I had left in my day to study for school.

It took me six years to graduate, and there were seasons when I had to lower the number of classes I was taking each semester to balance it all, but I still made it happen. It takes a strong why to get away from TV, video games, football, and whatever else is competing for your time. If you want to watch football more than prioritizing schoolwork or business tasks, you probably won't get the results you're looking for.

CHAPTER THREE

What Is Your Highest & Best Use?

> *"Success comes when we identify our natural talents and then work diligently to develop them into extraordinary skills."*
> **John C. Maxwell**

Something I learned while in college was a term known as the "highest and best use" principle. Typically, it's used in relation to real estate development and property value, but I'd like to expand on its definition and apply the same principle to people and businesses.

Knowing the highest and best use was something that came to be incredibly beneficial for me while in commercial real estate and business counseling over the years.

With a background in economics, business, and finance, we took this method learned in school and applied it to buildings and real estate. We'd look at a vacant lot or parcel and analyze what would be the highest and best use for this property. Basically, doing a feasibility study, looking at all the variables which could affect the ultimate value and return on investment, (ROI) of the property to its owner(s).

I've since applied those same principles I used in the real estate world and began applying them to people in terms of their best route for success in life.

The highest and best-use principle focuses on four fundamental criteria: legally permissible, physically possible, financially feasible, and maximally productive.

How I apply it when mentoring is simple: find out what you're good at and can make money doing.

It isn't simply what you like to do, because you can enjoy doing lots of things. But what do you excel in without having to really try hard? What is that thing that you are naturally good at?

If you're struggling to answer that, maybe it's something people always compliment you on or ask for advice and help with. It's a skill set you don't feel takes much effort, but people are amazed by your skills or knowledge in the area.

This is part of discovering your highest and best use.

Let me give you an example that I recently applied to someone's life.
I have a good friend. She's an engineer. We've talked regularly about her desire to develop a business outside of being an engineer. So, we're going over that exact principle.

I ask her, "So what are you good at?" And she dives into her love for fashion, getting dressed up nicely, and overall lifestyle fashion. So, I told her to focus on business ideas that relate to that area of her expertise. Something she enjoys and something she's good at.

She's a bodybuilder as well, even placing favorably in a few competitions. Sharing about health and exercise is something that she really enjoys. These passions of hers can provide her with several different career opportunities. Bodybuilding, health, nutrition and fashion could be morphed together to make one incredible hobby into a business idea.

Rather than trying to reinvent the wheel, spending years trying to develop a skill set that you don't even enjoy, how can you take something you already like and are naturally good at and amplify it? Don't worry about the things you know you aren't good at. Instead, focus on fine-tuning the areas where your natural skills match your natural interests.

I facilitated a class, and we discussed this very thing, and I will never forget the words, *"Don't worry about the things you're not good at because the best you could ever do is be average if that, or a little below average."* Although you can shape your skill sets and improve at something, it's a matter of the time you have to devote to development.

When looking at business opportunities you could start here and now or within the next few months, it's important to keep in mind your natural gifts. Sure, you can continue to develop in areas you aren't as skilled at, but at the end of the day, it's a matter of how quickly you want to get started in business.

My decision to buy a Carvel franchise store was a great example of seeing an opportunity and using my own highest and best use. At the time, this made the most sense because I had already worked in a Carvel store for three years while in high school. I knew the ins and outs of what it took to run the store and all the moving pieces from making the ice cream to maintaining cleanliness as required by the US Department of Agriculture and State Board of Health. The store was cleaned nightly, since I believed very strongly in keeping it sparkling!

Carvel tasks were like clockwork for me. All I needed to learn was the business back-office side, which eventually became muscle memory as well. Before I knew it, I had employees and was able to sit back a lot more and work on new skills in my free time.

Not only did I eventually get my bachelor's in economics, but I continued to read and improve myself. Although I wasn't necessarily applying these newfound skill sets within Carvel, I was honing in on new crafts for when the time came for a career change.

Over time, Carvel was no longer my highest and best use. I wasn't being challenged anymore, which left me feeling incredibly unfulfilled. I had accomplished the American dream but was still missing something. After feeling this way for several years, I decided to sell my store and head in a new direction, (something I go over more in a later chapter.

I ended up in commercial real estate, business investment, and insurance, and my experience and confidence in business grew. I had seen firsthand the rise and fall of the real estate market and how to pivot from there to stay successful in my own life. I had my fair share of learning experiences with starting and stopping business ventures, buying and selling businesses, and advising hundreds of people through the years.

All these experiences brought with them a newer highest and best use that I have maintained to this day with business mentorship.

Now, let's go back to those four criteria for highest and best use.

First, *being legally permissible. It should go without mentioning that your business needs to be legally sound.*

Every state has different laws and requirements to operate a business, so it's important to look into those laws or work alongside a legal professional and an accountant for this aspect of your business. They are the experts when it comes to both the regulation side of documentation and the financial aspect of running and owning a business.

Between a legal professional and a financial professional, you'll be able to get answers as to what documentation you'll need, if any, to start your business. They'll also be able to provide you with recommendations for running as a sole proprietor, LLC, or corporate level based on your business needs.

----

*The **second** is physically possible. This can mean several different things for different business ventures. It could relate to the time and energy you have towards creating and maintaining your business. It could also mean a literal location or your physical capability to provide the services.*

Have an honest conversation with yourself about your business idea (or ideas) and map out how realistic they are from a physical perspective. Consider ways that you could make it physically possible or other business ideas that might make more sense for where you're at right now. Keep in mind how it can still be shaped towards your longer-term goals.

----

*Financially feasible is the **third**. You can have legal set and ready to go, the physical means, but get stopped at the financial side of business. The good news is that there are many different grants, scholarships, business loans, and so much more out there.*

When considering your financial options, look at the investment compared to potential returns. This is where going back to the financial and legal professionals could be a good idea. Remember the pros and cons of slow growth, smaller business lines of credit, and loans.

While there are many opportunities to bring in funds to start a business, not all of them are good options. It will be on you, and any partners, to decide what the best move is financially and whether to start at a smaller, less costly stage or not. You might be at a different financial point in your life than another reader, which is why this has to be a more personalized decision.

Last *on the list is maximally productive. You need to look at your business, what you offer, where you offer it, and carefully evaluate current and future market estimates. Some things to consider include the demand for what you're offering, competition, and all potential income streams from this business.*

You've likely seen a shopping center that seems to always have a new for sale sign on its window. One business will grab it up, thinking they can be the change, only to move locations within a year.

This is a perfect example of the highest and best use, especially when it comes to being maximally productive. The location likely wasn't the right move, and had they done more market research before investing, they could be in a better spot.

In simple terms... what does it take to make a business successful?

It takes being realistic in the planning, expectations, and applications of business decisions, availability of funds, and good work ethics. Without these, a business will be set up for failure from the start. These three things are crucial for success.

Starting a business and maintaining a business takes a lot of grit. Reading through the highest and best use, and all the research needed to truly get a business going and being successful may not be appealing for everyone.

Balancing all the hats and completing all the tasks needed to be a successful business owner may sound too much for some.

Just know that you can have incredible skills and choose to stay working for another company. Business ownership offers a world of opportunities, but several people are living incredibly happy lives working for someone else.

It's okay to read through all the tasks needed and realize entrepreneurship isn't for you. It's also okay to give it a go and decide you prefer having a boss rather than being your own.

Let me share one more example of applying the highest and best use to entrepreneurship:

> *Years ago, I was helping people with buying and selling their companies. Well, one of these clients worked within the finance world and decided to open up a home services business he knew nothing about.*
>
> *What he did know really well was deep diving into the finances of this business. So, he decided he would purchase the company, pay a manager to run the home services and use his highest and best use to make it a more profitable business.*
>
> *Back in the day, someone interested in buying a company could do so with one-third financing. This meant that the owner would get paid one-third of the purchase price, and the remaining two-thirds would be owner-financed. As an example, someone could buy a $300,000 business with $100,000 down and a $200,000 note owed to the owner, essentially the same as owing money to the bank.*
>
> *Because of this client's background, he was able to increase prices, pay off the remaining debt owed to the original owner for buying the company, and start making extra gains.*

What a perfect example of being an entrepreneur while keeping to your natural skill sets. This client didn't pretend like he knew how to do the home services. If he did, he likely would have spread himself too thin to prioritize doing a price survey.

Had he not done a price survey, he wouldn't have realized that the services being provided were priced well under the market price range. Because of his focus on the highest and best use, he was able to raise the prices, maintain a team, and still profit.

You don't have to completely change what you're doing. You can open a business and task out the rest to people who are better skilled in these areas. That's one of the smartest things you can do as a business owner.

CHAPTER FOUR

The Value Of Drilling

> "When all is said and done,
> more is said than done."
> **Lou Holtz**

Drilling is important for success, and no, I don't mean oil. There's a phrase that gets thrown around a lot about how practice makes perfect, but that's rarely the actual case. A more accurate expectancy is that practice makes progress.

The military is a field that is constantly drilling. Soldiers go through training on a regular basis to prepare for potential real-world scenarios. They do this so that when the real conflicts come up, they are prepared and have this muscle memory already built up.

These drills also allow soldiers to test different battle plans in a mock scenario instead of trying it in real life first. It gives the team a chance to learn how to best work together too. The same principle applies to the civilian world.

The longer I'm in the business world helping with mentoring and consulting, the more I see the importance of drilling. From prepping before an important meeting or phone call, to working with a new client. Practicing helps us hone in on our craft and prepare for potential issues that might arise within the comfort of a mock scenario before diving into reality.

My motto is: If it's important enough to do, it's important enough to drill.

One of the best ways to practice drilling is with another person or a group of individuals. Ideally, someone that you know will be honest with you. Practice with someone who will give a well-rounded critique, not simply tell you that you did a good job.

Drilling provides an opportunity for us to improve our craft in a situation that is much more accepting of mistakes that are made. Errors can be looked at, and improvements made, before heading into the experience with outsiders that might not be as accepting.

There are many ways to go about these practices. Visualization is one. Brainstorm different scenarios or have an acquaintance work alongside you. Consider several different obstacles that could come up. How can you work with those obstacles smoothly?

Another way is by doing recordings of yourself. This can be in the form of an audio message or actual video recordings. Either way, this process of drilling allows you to see how your body language is, your tone of voice, and pick up on areas you can improve in.

Mock sessions are another great way to practice drilling. This will need to be done with a partner, or multiple individuals, but it allows for a mock round of whatever situation you're preparing for in your business or work environment.

Remember: Drilling doesn't mean you'll be perfect.

You could still go into the situation and errors might come up, generally, things are very much out of your control. Do your best to not let this get you down. Practice makes improvement, it doesn't make perfect.

Let me share an example from the corporate side of drilling.

> *I was advising someone who works for a college. He had ten years of experience, a master's degree, and a number of credentials, and was ready for a change in position within the field. Really, it was time for him to start making more money in his career.*
>
> *At the time he was making around $85,000. He was eying a new job opportunity that could bring in $125,000 at the highest salary range. So, I told him it was time to drill.*
>
> *The first thing for drilling came with a negotiation practice. I asked him to give me the facts first.*
>
> *The facts were that the current organization could give him $110,000 at most for another department. His other option was to work within his current department and ask for an increase to $100,000.*
>
> *One determining factor in working in a different department was the amount of work stress that would follow due to the mess he'd have*

to fix for at least the next year. He had to decide if the increase in income would be worth the year of stress, or if it'd be better to simply ask for a pay raise in his current department.

So, we drilled on asking for more money in his current department. He learned about the different salaries that others had within a similar role that he was holding. We went over his current benefits to the department, and how to highlight that.

Next was the big ask. Putting in a bid for the salary he wanted to have and seeing what the department was able to work with him on. He shared the new role he was offered as an added incentive for raising his salary to keep him.

After practicing the interview, getting offered the new position, and negotiating with his current department, he was able to receive a $15,000 annual salary increase in a field he was incredibly happy in.

Why? Because he asked.

Here's another example. There was a guest speaker who shared a story about his time working for a radio or TV station. I'm not sure which one, and it's not that important to the story. Anyway, he had been working for this station for some time. His job at the time was very innocuous and mediocre. What he really wanted was to get into broadcasting for the organization.

What happened? He practiced all the time when no one was around. He'd practice how he'd say things, what he'd do, etc. He would practice for a long time each day.

Well, one day the regular guy called in sick and couldn't show up. The producer asked him to go through a list of people and see who was most qualified and available to replace the regular guy.

The person went through the list and told his boss, "No one else is available, but I can do it. I've been practicing."

Not only did his hard work at drilling pay off for landing that *substitute position, but he did such a good job that his boss gave him a job.*

The moral of the story? "It's better to be prepared for an opportunity and not have one, than to have an opportunity and not be prepared." - Les Brown
Note: I heard him live on one of my many trips. He's phenomenal!

You need to act as if you already have the opportunity you want, which means regularly drilling. This will help you stand out and can ultimately land you your dream gig.

Another example I'll share relates to gaining partnerships with larger businesses. For the last few weeks, I've been drilling for a big conference call. My business partner and I will go back and forth as if we are at the conference already. Getting this deal with the larger business would be a huge step towards our long-term goals and offerings.

So how are we applying drilling? First was putting together a checklist of all the things we need to be aware of. The biggest is making up what kind of problems could happen. These are essentially mock scenarios for us to practice. Who might come along and kill the deal the last go around? What's the personality of the people in the room? Where'd they go to school? What was their upbringing like?

Part of the drilling process includes researching who they are before even meeting. It's like watching *CSI (Crime Scene Investigation)* when they're profiling someone. We want to know as much about this person and the organization as possible. What companies are they connected with? What topics should we bring up? Which topics should we avoid? The more scenarios and details you can gather the better your drilling practice will be.

What happens when you don't drill?

Boy, do I have several "shoulda, coulda" moments over the last 50+ years of entrepreneurship. One example of how things didn't pan out as planned was opening a convenience-like store on the same lot as the Carvel was on. I did zero preparation, including drilling and getting advice, before spending thousands of dollars (big money back then) to start this new business.

To be frank with you, it was a stupid idea. I never should have done it. But because I felt like this hotshot business owner, I didn't take the time to research. Had I drilled some different scenarios around buying this convenience store, asked for advice, really anything... I would have been in a much better situation. Like, not even buying it to begin with.

Sometimes you do well and sometimes you wish you had done more homework! Sometimes you win, sometimes you lose. There are times when you have to make poor decisions to learn to never make those types of decisions ever again.

A huge reason why I wrote this book was so that you can learn from me and my poor choices, rather than making costly mistakes on your own.

Entrepreneurship requires the ability to make changes. Things can change overnight; you need to be ready to go.

Are you ready for change?

Have you developed the skills needed to enable you to be successful as an entrepreneur? Or... Are you just pipe dreaming? If you need more skills, get the skills first before taking the leap.

Drilling is a great tool for helping you see if you still have areas to improve in, or if you're ready to go!

Chapter Five

Build Your Support System

> *"Ah, but I was so much older then,*
> *I'm younger than that now."*
> **Bob Dylan, My Back Pages**

It took me nearly losing it all to truly realize the importance of having a support system. I had already sold my Carvel Franchise at this point in my life. I jumped into start-up ideas that didn't end well.

I was lost, without money, and poor in spirit... unsure of how I would be able to provide for my family in this new chapter of our lives.

One day I ran into an acquaintance from my church and started to see the true value of mentorship. This guy saw my circumstances, asked me what I was going to do about it, and opened my eyes to a new world of opportunity in business.

He was working in the business investment and commercial real estate field. It was something I hadn't put too much thought into, but it later became a profession I have worked in for much of my working life after this point.

Not all mentors are good mentors.

A good mentor will be able to help you navigate business challenges. They'll counsel you to look from an outside perspective to come up with the best solution on your own through their guidance and support. They can also be someone who assists you in developing new skill sets and knowledge and be an asset in not only your career but your life as well.

When looking into mentorship options, keep in mind that they should help keep you level-headed, with a balance of exploration and realism. If a potential mentor is offering you "the moon and all the stars" for your business, they are likely full of it. Though you can achieve amazing success, there are a lot of "get-rich-quick schemes" out there, and it's important to keep that in mind when connecting with a potential mentor.

A good mentor will call you out when needed. They'll also expect you to act. If you are given suggestions, they will be looking to see how well you respond to the information you're provided. Pending this being a paid mentor or someone volunteering their time, they may quickly decide to no longer help if they aren't seeing you putting forth equal effort.

So how can you get the most from a mentor?

If I'm honest, part of my lack of success can be attributed to my lack of mentorship. This was an area of weakness for me for many years. Having someone who had already been in my shoes before but had leveled up would have helped me so much in my earlier years. But I simply didn't understand the importance of them. It was my pride that blocked me.

Having a business mentor would have helped me with some of the tough decisions I made in my life, like opening a convenience store without proper research, or selling my Carvel store before I had anything else set in place. I didn't realize the need when I was younger because I was "already a businessman, why would I need the advice?" but oh was I wrong.

One of the biggest things to consider is what that person specializes in. They should be strong in an area you're weak in. What is their expertise? Be sure to look at what they know and real-life experiences, not just showy representation. Another consideration is testimonials from others who have previously worked with this person. What growth did they experience in their business and/or personal life?

If all looks good, the next step would be to schedule a one-on-one meeting with them to ensure your personalities mesh, and that you're comfortable with their style of mentoring. If things don't align, there will be other opportunities.

Keep in mind that a mentor can be labeled as many different things. Some additional names include advisor, coach, and consultant. Many of which will be individuals you pay to work with. These individuals can help you with setting goals, developing an action plan for said goals, and providing added accountability for reaching those listed goals.

The choice is yours for whether you feel having a mentor can benefit your situation, but many will say they wouldn't be where they are today in business had it not been for the help of someone else. Many mentors have been where you are right now, so they will do their best to ensure you don't fall down the same holes they did.

Up next in building a support system: networking opportunities

----

There are so many different affiliations or organizations that can be found relating to your area of work or passions.

Regardless of the field of work, everyone within an organization has something they can bring to the table. The importance is building a support system of like-minded individuals.

It wasn't until my late twenties to early thirties that I realized the importance of this and started joining several organizations to gain exposure and experience. I volunteered for several different organizations such as Nonprofit Service Groups, Toast Masters, etc.

I knew that part of my job as a successful entrepreneur was learning how to communicate with people and present well. These service clubs helped in developing my character and business skills that I otherwise wouldn't have experienced had I not belonged to different organizations. The networking opportunities have also been a game changer.

Organizations like Bunker Labs, the Southern Nevada Veteran Chamber of Commerce, and the Veterans of Foreign Wars (VFW) have been game changers when it came to my success and support.

Bunker Labs is a nationwide business incubator for veterans and veteran spouses. Helping them with tools and resources to be successful in business. From my six months with Bunker Labs alone, I was able to meet so many incredible people who were able to introduce me to others within their own circle.

One of those individuals was Monica Fullerton (Founder/CEO, @Spouse-Ly). If it wasn't for that connection at Bunker Labs, I wouldn't have been able to get connected with Melissa Anne, a big help to me with this book.

Had it not been for one of my close friends' daughters, Savannah Grace Newman, a college student, I would still be in the thought stage of this book and not getting anything on paper. It would have just been notes. I would still be stuck in the framework of writing. I needed a team to help me get from just some idea to the completed project you have right now.

Always be teachable.

Something to keep in mind with networking and growing connections is that you can always be the student. It doesn't matter how old you are, how young they are, or how much experience you have. Sometimes the role will be reversed, and the mentor will become the mentee.

Don't be so prideful in thinking you have everything figured out that you can't learn from someone else. If I had been, I wouldn't be where I am today.

Even Mr. Carvel himself sat in a room with a team of franchise owners, me included, to get recommendations and insights. You should never allow yourself to get so big that you don't think you need to get feedback from others.

A benefit of having a support system with business is having people you can go to for advice. Even Mr. Tom Carvel, founder of the Carvel Ice Cream Company, himself did this with his ice cream franchise owners, and I have done it many times over the years with my own business move decisions.

Choosing your team of advisors.

I had considered moving away from running one of my businesses as my main priority. Instead of sitting in my head about it, I took it to my support system for outside perspectives.

I said something like, "*Listen... here's my dilemma. I'm burned out in this field. I make good money off it, but it's not my highest and best use. These are the things I am passionate about, and really good at. What should I do?*" And you know what? I got a lot of good advice.

One friend shared something along the lines of, "*Life is short. Why not do what you want with the years you have left? Build a business around what you truly enjoy.*" So, I did. I decided to shift my priorities.

Having a team of advisors doesn't just apply to business decisions either. It can benefit the corporate side of work too. For example, I was speaking with a highly skilled medical professional about their job.

They were ready to accept a position without making a salary comparison. Had I not done the research to compare them for this person and brought up their options, they would have been missing out on making $75,000 to $80,000 more per year.

So how do you find the people to get advice from to begin with? You can start by joining organizations. Nonprofits are a great option to join because they usually don't charge. Many of these nonprofit organizations offer everything from classes to cohorts and even seminars.

Bunker Labs, a nationwide business organization open to military veterans and their spouses, helps existing businesses to take things to the next level and it was one I benefited from heavily. I initially joined because I wanted to learn about social media, analyzing traffic, and everything else relating to the digital world of business. The connections I built were even more beneficial, as I shared earlier.

My business partner also found great success from attending different seminars over the years. He built a support system for both the seminar attendees and those that taught the different educational pieces. He has built phenomenal support with people from all walks of life. Not just those in business, but people he respects. These are people he has been able to trust opinions of when it comes to running ideas past them.

If you don't have a support system, you likely won't have as much success as you could have had. But it is also important not to have an echo chamber of support. Having people with different viewpoints and chapters of life can provide alternative ways of thinking that you would likely be unable to do alone. Keep in mind that you don't necessarily have to take it to heart, but to have genuine outlooks from others is priceless.

CHAPTER SIX

Don't Be Deceived By Time

> "Experience is the hardest kind of teacher.
> It gives you the test first and the lesson afterward."
> **Oscar Wilde**

Just because you've been doing something for a long time doesn't mean you're growing. When I purchased the Carvel Franchise, I had already spent several years working in a semi-managerial position before taking on the title of Franchise owner.

At some point, most of the tasks became autopilot for me. But I still felt like a hot shot, especially once I was able to start affording amazing vacations, and a beautiful home. So, in my mind, I was a great business owner.

Unfortunately, seven years of business doesn't always mean seven years of business experience. So, when my hotshot self decided to sell my Carvel franchise, I quickly learned that I didn't know nearly enough about business.

You see, owning a franchise is very different than starting a business from scratch.

Though you can be successful in either of the two, when you own a franchise, you're handed a tried-and-true handbook to help you succeed as a new owner. This isn't the case for many other areas of business.

In my mind, I had seven years of experience in the world of business. It turned out I just had one year of business multiplied by seven. You might be thinking, "*Dennis, isn't that the same thing?*" and my answer would be, "*Heck no!*"

You see, seven years of business experience means that you've experienced different situations and overcome them over those seven years. Seven years of experience means gaining knowledge and skill sets in a vast array of business-related circumstances.

Nothing really changed after the first year when I owned my franchise. Once I learned the ropes, everything else stayed repetitive over those seven years. Most things were provided to me by the franchisor, Carvel Corporation.

So, when it came time for me to make my own business decisions after selling the store, I quickly became aware how much I still had to study up on if I wanted to be successful in business again.

Even before selling Carvel, I made my fair share of mistakes. One of which was when I opened the convenience store next to the Carvel Store, previously mentioned earlier. It was totally out of my element. I had no idea what I was doing and really had no right to waste my resources doing so. I wasn't prepared.

I had zero knowledge of how to analyze business, or really what even went into having a convenience store to begin with. I simply went with the idea with minimal research, lost a ton of money, and it blew up in my face.

How can you become more prepared?

This goes back to the self-examination. Looking at your skill sets. Do you have the necessary skills to accomplish this goal? Like when I was thinking about going to medical school.

My father said, "*Hey, that's something you choose long in advance... are you prepared mentally, financially, with your family, to do this? If you're going to be in business too, you're going to be away a lot. Have you really thought this through or is it just an impulse? Did you really give any thought to this thing?*"

Starting a new venture sounds fun. It's thrilling and can be a big stroke to the ego to say we're going to pursue this new thing. But if we aren't smart about it, we can quickly lose our stability and spiral way down. We might be better off without pursuing it.

I'll give an example of a couple that was getting ready to retire. They chose to invest their life savings into opening a restaurant. Never been in business before, but they wanted to pursue it anyway. Why? Because they had these wonderful recipes from Grandma that they thought would be great for starting a business.

There was nothing truly unique to their offer, and they had no idea how much truly went into running a restaurant.

They lost their entire savings, shed a lot of tears, and ultimately the husband had to go back to work in his 60s. Money that could have been used to have a nice retirement turned into nothing because they didn't do the prep and inner reflection necessary to see if this was even a good idea from the start.

So many people are looking to hit a home run. How about just shooting a single?

Hitting a home run is not likely to happen. While it's great to think positively, you still have to be realistic. You can't live with your head in the cloud and walk around like that.

Your opportunity is to be a niche that makes sense to others. It has to be something people are going to buy. Not just some great idea that played in your head that you didn't do any research on before going all in. What makes your offer unique? What secret sauce is in your business that will make people want to come to you over someone else?

I can remember reading something from Rich DeVos, founder of Amway. And he said something like, "*Do you know why Amway sells soap? The reason why Amway sells soap is because people buy soap.*"

If research isn't your strong suit, that's okay.

Every avenue of business will require different skill sets. In some areas, you can choose to hire someone more qualified than you. This generally isn't something you can do at the start when you're bootstrapping and funding your business out of pocket though. It's on you as a business owner to make the best financial decision in this area.

If you aren't at a point where you can hire an expert in that field, and even if you are, it's important to gain a basic level of understanding in these different areas to better set yourself and your business up for success.

Formal education can be helpful, but learning from business experience is crucial. You should never stop learning. There will always be new trends, new marketing platforms, social media, changes in the financial world, and new laws that come into place that will affect your business.

The brevity of time.

There's a quote I remember hearing from Billy Graham that has stuck with me for many years. I believe it was part of an interview. Someone was asking him what was most impacting out of all the things he had done in his lifetime. His response? *"The greatest surprise in my life is the brevity of life. Time is the capital we've been given by God to invest wisely. Make the Most of every opportunity because the brevity of time calls for immediate action."* How will you keep this in mind within your own life?

Consider when you've said something along the lines of, *"I'm just not quite ready yet,"* or *"I'll start doing that soon,"* only for years to pass you by in the process.

If you don't set up something that's date and time-specific, it's likely not going to happen. All too often it's just talk. Keep in mind that we think we have all the time in the world. We don't.

"It's already taken me six months, and I haven't made a sale yet?!"

But don't get it twisted. Although our moments are limited, it's important to remember that things can and do still take precious time. It's a process to grow a business. Much of it can take three, four, or even five years before you start to see the fruit of your labor.

Real estate is a great example of this. It could take years before making a profit or sale. A relationship is another example of something which takes years to develop and attain a healthy balance of success and growth. Hasn't it been said repeatedly that good things come to those who wait? My caveat would be to those who wait and to those who plan. Having been married for 50+ years, I can attest to this wholeheartedly.

Don't forget to look at the long game too, not just the short game.

CHAPTER SEVEN

What Thoughts Are You Repeating?

> *"If you don't like something, change it.
> If you can't change it, change your attitude."*
> **Maya Angelou**

Our thoughts are powerful. They're especially powerful when they are regularly repeated to ourselves. This can be both in the positive thinking sort of way or the negative. What you think will heavily impact how you show up in business.

What thoughts are you repeating to yourself? Are you looking at all the ways you can fail? How many other businesses aren't making it? Or are you looking at the opportunities to succeed? Why are these other businesses successful?

The truth is that negative thoughts aren't necessarily bad. Knowing all the ways you could potentially fail can be incredibly beneficial. Analyzing what other businesses are doing so you don't do what they did is also helpful. However, it is only helpful if you're able to look at those scenarios and find a positive outcome.

For example, if you can picture one way that your business could fail... what actions can you perform? What connections can you make? What can you do to help solve this problem?

How we think can shape our perspective on the world and influence how we show up in it. It can easily trap us in cycles of pessimism, fear, and self-doubt. All things that can keep us from reaching our potential.

Though these thoughts tend to be automatic and subconscious beliefs and patterns, we do have the capability of shifting our perspective with practice. One of the first steps is becoming aware of the negative thought patterns you may have. The next step is questioning those thoughts.

How can you reframe this thought into something more positive, productive, or realistic? How can you provide yourself with compassion for thinking said thoughts? And how can you focus on more positive thoughts?

Negative thinking can heavily hinder not only our business success but our personal growth and well-being. It's on us to work on retraining our minds to be more positive.

Along my business journey, I was involved with many different businesses. Many were not financially successful, but each of them taught me a lesson. I did, however, notice how negative my thought patterns had been getting. I can remember one day when I was feeling so sick.

I was lying on my leather recliner feeling sick to my stomach with nausea and as I closed my eyes, I realized that all I was thinking about was sickness. So, I started saying things like, "*I feel great, wonderful. It's a beautiful day out there,*" and I talked myself out of being sick.

A lot of times our mind goes to the negative and we have to retrain the brain.

My negative patterns got to the point where I almost gave up on success, continuously thinking that I was not going to make it. I had stinkin' thinkin'. So, you might be wondering, as I did, how exactly do I get rid of this?

I grew up like many of you, with a father who wasn't trained in Great Parenting 101. Quite frankly, it was the opposite.

He was taught by his older brothers, (I assume) how to discipline the male sons in the family. The philosophy was to criticize them, and they will internally say to themselves, "*Ok, I'll show you*" and magically become a better person.

Obviously, that type of parenting doesn't usually work. In my case it backfired.

My father was not very encouraging to me, like he was to my sister. He lavished her with praise and encouragement. It seemed like we had different fathers (we didn't.).

As the recipient of his parenting/teaching style, it showed in so many areas.

For example, little league baseball. If I missed an opportunity, a play, he would chew me out right on the field, in front of all the players.

Another example, I was having a hard time learning about a specific algebra problem and asked my father to help me. When I didn't catch on, he got so mad, he threw the papers at me and called me self-defeating words. Naturally, that does wonders for your self-esteem... not.

I won't bore you with the hundreds of other episodes, but I think you get the picture. Long story short, I struggled with self-esteem issues for many years. Believing everything I had accomplished in life, excelling in so many aspects of life and business, it was all by luck.

Even graduating from college was because I had all easy teachers and classes. Common really.

Did you really believe the lies? I'm sorry to say that I did. Well, how did I pull myself out of the "muddy water?"

While I was doing self-analysis, reading a lot of books, I came across one titled, "What To Say When You Talk To Yourself[2]," written by Shad Helmstetter. In his book he described, in detail, some of the issues I was dealing with.

For example, "*I'm not good enough... I can't take on a higher challenge... I am not really a smart person, I am unworthy,*" etc.

I was confronted with my own negative self-talk, and it was ugly.

My road to recovery started right then and there. Determined to change my mind set, I started working on my self-talk.

One way to work on this is by speaking with a close friend or someone you trust the opinion of, together you can hold one another accountable and keep track of your thoughts. I was shocked by how much negativity I had coming out of my own brain.

So, I started to work on my inner dialogue. I used to have a bunch of little notes on 5x7 cards with all sorts of positive thoughts written down. That stack of cards would come with me everywhere I went for weeks, maybe even months. Every day, many times I would read and re-read the cards. If I started going down that rabbit hole, I would immediately stop the negative self-talk and start repeating hundreds of positive, encouraging words to myself. Fortunately, after a while, I noticed my brain was starting to shift and wasn't entertaining as many negative thoughts and emotions as in the past. For me it was a revelation and gratefully, after so many months, the transformation of my thinking had taken hold.

After all these years, I have replaced the negative self-talk with positive self-talk, and I have helped many other folks learn, deal, and change their self-talk. Like Forrest Gump would say, "*That's all I've got to say about that.*"

"Just one small positive thought in the morning can change your whole day." Dalai Lama

---

Mental imaging is another important way to reshape our thoughts. I remember being around nine years old. My uncle and grandma lived on a cul-de-sac with a pond nearby. In the winter it would freeze over.

One Sunday afternoon they brought an extra pair of ice skates for me to go out and skate with them. I couldn't get upright to save my life. Every time I got up, I went straight back down. My whole body hurt.

Ever since that event, I would visualize myself skating around the pond with no problem. Fast forward 30 or 35 years later, I had my second opportunity to ice skate at a church function. There were a couple hundred of us there and everyone was asking if I would be ice skating. I put on skates and went around almost doing tricks.

People were like, "*How the heck are you able to do this? You're really good!*" It was my first time being able to ice skate. How do you explain that? I had skated already a thousand times in my head.

A similar story relating to the power of our mental visualization. One guy was super big on golfing, but he hadn't done it in six years due to being a prisoner of war (POW) in North Vietnam. When he was brought back to the United States and was able to get back on a golf course, he was just as good if not better than the last time he had played. All because he had visualized golfing over those years as a POW.

What is something you'd like to be good at but aren't right now? How can you begin visualizing this change in skill set? What does it feel like to be this new person?

There is a lot that is stored subconsciously that we aren't even aware of. These things will pop up into our conscious mind, and it can take time to work through why they are there and where they came from.

By learning how best to challenge these negative thoughts and bring out a more positive mindset, you will begin to feel more empowered and create a fulfilling life.

You are a lot more powerful than your thoughts might make you feel.

You have the power to change your thoughts and transform your reality but don't forget to give yourself a lot of grace along the way. Sometimes we are brutal with ourselves and make life a lot more difficult. We can be condemning and a lot of it comes from how we were brought up. Whether it was from growing up in a negative atmosphere with constant criticism as kids and not much positive nurturing. Maybe you weren't ever encouraged through the years, never complimented or told you were doing a good job by those you looked up to.

Whatever it might have been, if you're like me, it leaves you with low self-esteem and self-condemnation. Those things last for a long time.

It took me until around 40 years old to realize I was brought up that way, and it took me a lot of time to work on how I processed things.

Remember that it's a journey. Where you are right now doesn't have to be where you stay. Though life will always have challenges, there are opportunities for support along the way.

Be open to opportunities.
What does that even mean though?

One way of being open to opportunities is not being afraid to ask. A lot of people are too afraid, or insecure, to ask for things in life. This can be practiced in big and small ways.

Practicing with the small things can help you work past the repeating thoughts that might be keeping you from new opportunities. Let me share a few examples, some silly little things, some incredible.

The first is on the fast-food lines. I've been training my grandkids not to be afraid to ask, so when we go through the fast-food lines we'll ask, "are you sampling anything today?" I mean, how many people ask that? But it's gotten us things like free hamburgers, French fries, and ice cream cones.

Another example is a little bigger deal. Since I maintained my private pilot license, I would periodically go out to the Henderson, Nevada Executive Airport. One day I was there with a friend and fellow private pilot license holder to see a new high-performance single-engine Mooney.

While we were there, I noticed several folks were coming into the hangar from the rear door. Of course, being the curious person that I am, I had to ask the pilot where he was coming from.

He shared about his flight coming from the Grand Canyon and how he needed to head back in an hour for the passengers. Half-jokingly, I asked if he had any room, and he said, "Sure!" So, my buddy and I got to ride with him back to pick up the passengers.

Since my buddy was a better pilot than I was, he was able to sit on the right seat next to the pilot and we gained a free ride around the Grand Canyon.

My wife and some of our friends would go out for St. Patrick's Day dinner. I got a delicious stew at a restaurant on St. Patrick's Day one year. It might have embarrassed my wife, but I saw this woman behind us at dinner that had the same Irish stew I had. It was so enjoyable that I wanted more. I noticed that this woman hadn't finished hers, so I turned around and said, "*I have two questions for you. One, would you mind if I finished your stew, and two, would you loan me five bucks?*" She said, "*I'll give you the stew, but not the five bucks.*" and we both laughed. My wife didn't think it was funny. My wife and friends were embarrassed, but I had a good time.

I got free items from fast-food restaurants, a free flight around the Grand Canyon, and a great laugh about the delicious stew, among numerous other opportunities over the years. Why? Because I asked. Don't ever be afraid to ask. I have never had anyone get mad at me or retaliate for asking.

I'll give one more example. Someone I knew who was working in a corporate environment. She was underpaid and desired appropriate compensation. Instead of waiting and hoping that her boss would notice and choose to pay her more, she asked. Because she wasn't afraid to ask, she was able to get a 30% raise.

Can you imagine what a 30% increase in your income would do for you? Look for ways to point out your strengths, and don't be afraid to ask if you know you deserve more.

Working on mindset shifts and changing the repeating negative behaviors that aren't rendering the results we want to see in our lives are crucial to success. Not just entrepreneurial, but in our everyday lives as well.

How are you talking to yourself?

Our inner dialogue is so important it's worth repeating some specifics here. When looking at someone going into business, I like to ask about their self-talk. What kind of thoughts are you saying to yourself? If you can't think of anything specific, what do you find yourself focusing on?

I found for myself I was focused on negativity. Many of the individuals I consult for business are the same. One of the biggest comes with excuses and negative outlooks on their success.

They'll give five excuses for why it won't work without being able to give five reasons why it can. They only see obstacles, so I have to help them see the five positives. They have a hard time visualizing it because they're so focused on all the negativity in their brain.

What do you say when you talk to yourself? It helped me after selling my Carvel Franchise and failing at my first go-around of business. I had all this junk in my head and had to fight it. It was a real internal battle. But I made it through, and you can too.

If you continue in self-destructive inner dialogue, then you're going to have a difficult time in life and business.

CHAPTER EIGHT

Should You Stay Or Should You Go?

> *"Follow your passion - and if you don't know what it is, realize that one reason for your existence on earth is to find it."*
> **Oprah Winfrey**

Don't be afraid to change your mind. I always thought I wanted to be a pilot. Just after graduating from high school, I would drive out to Long Island, New York to take flying lessons at Zahn's Airport, a private airfield located in North Amityville, Long Island, NY, which operated from 1936-1980.

Upon completion of my flight hours and receiving my private license, flying around Long Island and New York City became a favorite pastime. The views from the air were incredible, and something only few have experienced. I would watch planes take off and land at Kennedy Airport, imagining it being me flying the planes, wondering what cities they were going to and imagining what a great career this could be.

At this time, I felt like getting my private license was one of the best decisions I'd ever made. I truly thought I'd found my calling in the aviation field and even pursued it when I served my country in the Army. While stationed in Germany, I got to explore the scenery of the German countryside, and I loved it.

After being honorably discharged from the service, I decided to continue my path through aviation, by applying and getting accepted to Embry-Riddle Aeronautical University in Daytona Beach, Florida.

Embry-Riddle was probably one of the most prominent aviation universities in the United States. The tuition to attend this school was through the roof, but it would be worth it, because I would end up getting all the different pilot ratings I needed, as well as earning a degree in aeronautical science. This program was one of the best out there, at the time, to prepare me for a future in aviation as a commercial airline pilot. Or so I thought.

On a very hot and humid summer day in 1972, everything changed.

As I was practicing some of the many aviation maneuvers, (for example: Touch & Go landings and stalls), with my instructor next to me, I started feeling nauseous. I don't know if it was from the Daytona Beach humidity and heat, or the odd maneuvers I encountered while flying, but I was feeling miserable.

Thankfully there was a storm coming, so we decided to pull off to the taxi way and wait for the thunderstorm to pass as was very common in Daytona Beach during the summertime. As we waited, I remember talking to my instructor and I asked, "am I supposed to be enjoying this?"

His response was along the lines of "*learning how to fly is not as fun as flying but should still be enjoyable*".

Because of my body's reactions to some of the maneuvers, we ended up heading to the Chief Pilot's office at Embry Riddle to talk about my options moving forward.

There were two real directions. Continue with a four-year degree and be bogged down with student loan debt or withdraw from the program. This was an era just after the Vietnam War, where airlines were being inundated by more qualified applicants from the Air Force, Army, Marines, and Navy, with way more flight hours than students would have coming from the program I was in. Bottom line - the competition was fierce, unlike today, where we have shortages of pilots and airlines desperate for skilled aviators.

After some reflection, I made the decision to withdraw from the program, which terminated my professional aviation career. Flying had been an exciting hobby for me, something I enjoyed getting to do on my own terms. Like flying around New York or Germany when the weather was perfect and the views were beautiful. It helped me quickly realize the competitive environment and lack of freedom in the air was not for me.

When considering whether to stay or go, you have to ask yourself, "Is this just a fun pastime or possible occupation that you can do under all circumstances?"

Sometimes you don't know until you know. It wasn't until I was in my program that I realized it wasn't the right move for me. I trusted my gut feeling and moved back home to New York instead of pursuing a commercial pilot career.

Many times in life, trusting your gut is a wise decision.

Learning to differentiate anxiety, fear, and intuition will make a huge difference in your decision-making processes. I've relied on my gut feeling hundreds of times over 50 years, and it's served me well.

For example, my closest friend worked for a successful Wall Street startup that went on to become a multi-billion-dollar company. The founder would say, "*Trust and go with your gut. It's right in most cases.*"

I still had my license for flying smaller planes, so back home I could visit the Long Island airport and rent a plane to fly around with for a few hours before coming back home. During one of my visits to the flight line, I started talking with an instructor pilot and discovered that he had graduated with the same degree I was pursuing at Embry Riddle.

Turned out, he had tens of thousands of dollars in student loans he was paying off and was working as a flight instructor, barely over minimum wage. That conversation helped me realize that I made the right decision for me in choosing to end my professional flying career path.

Are you feeling stuck?

Maybe you aren't looking to go to school. Maybe you're in the thick of it with your current professional circumstances and stuck on whether you should stay with that job or seek out alternatives.

Here are a few questions to ask yourself, that I hope can help you with that important decision:

Are you feeling sick about a situation you're in? (Maybe not literally sick, but something just isn't sitting right.) Maybe it's a living situation, or a career choice. Could it be your intuition telling you something? (Intuition, also known as your gut.)

If you could start all over again, would you still be doing what you're doing now? Why or why not? Maybe you simply need an adjustment in your business, but maybe it's time to pursue other directions.

What if...

In what ways would you change your direction if you knew you could succeed? It can be hard to tell if it's a fear-based decision due to uncertainties, or a knowing that this simply isn't right for you. Remember to trust your internal instincts.

It's okay to change your mind. Sometimes quitting is the wisest decision. It doesn't mean you failed, as long as you tried, and got some sort of result. Even if failure seems inevitable, you never truly fail if you've learned from the experience. When something doesn't feel right, it usually isn't.

Be open to redirection and new opportunities. This is where mentorship becomes really important. Speak with friends, and family, and share your feelings. You might just be surprised at how their input can be of value to you.

Deciding to sell my Carvel franchise was a massive business decision for me. It was my "should I stay or should I go" moment. You can be incredibly successful and still decide to leave.

This goes back to leaning into your instincts. If something doesn't feel right, dig a little deeper. Reflect on why your mind and body are feeling this way regarding this specific circumstance.

A few years after selling Carvel, my family and I began moving a lot. We left the New York winters behind, and we were so grateful for that. Unfortunately, after ten years living in the scorching heat of

Scottsdale, Arizona, we realized that summertime was not for us either, so we headed off to San Diego.

Career-wise, while living in Arizona, I began working in the commercial real estate and business advising industry. Around the time of our move to California, I was ready for another career change, because commercial real estate was just not doing it for me anymore. I didn't enjoy the day-to-day activities.

Once we arrived in San Diego, I came across an ad for professionals in marketing for insurance and other financial services. The name of the company triggered a memory from my youth of a TV series called 'Mutual of Omaha's Wild Kingdom'. I realized this company must be doing something right to still be profitable many years later.

I reached out, took all the tests that were required of me, and started working with them as an independent contractor. This was one of the best decisions I have ever made for myself. I'm still working with them and other financial institutions to this day, working a flexible schedule as I desire.

Real examples of 'stay or go'

A medical professional talked about getting out of the corporate hospital side of the field and starting their own practice. The decision took this person years, likely because of a few mental blocks: the fear of the unknown, fear of being incapable of succeeding and fear that they were becoming a business owner and not a medical professional.

You know what happened once he stepped out and started his practice? He's now making twice his original income and not having to work as many hours. He now has a team working under him and is looking to continue expanding his business.

He could have let these fears keep him from pushing forward. Instead, he took a chance, and it turned out to be incredibly favorable for him.

Another example was someone considering discharging from the military. They had already served eight or nine years when we started talking about his transition to civilian life, and he was torn about doing another 12 years.

I simply asked, "do you know what you'll be making by staying in until you've served 20 years?" He didn't have an answer for me, so I said, "let's take out a calculator and find out."

Considering inflation, they would give up thousands of dollars in retirement and their financial security. We also looked at the average salary in the civilian world, and we discovered he would be better off financially if he remained in the military. The positives outweighed the negatives.

The last example is a discussion with property owners in Southern California about 25 years ago. Two individuals were split over selling or keeping a rental property. We discussed the current status of the real estate market and analyzed the pros and cons of each decision. The chief complaint seemed to be that the property needed additional maintenance and upkeep that had not been initially accounted for.

The partners chose to hold out the sale for a little longer and put some money into the work needed. As a result of this decision, a year later they were able to sell the property for an $85,000 profit. When I asked them if it was worth it after they got the check, their immediate response was a resounding 'yes'.

Ultimately, the decision to stay or go is entirely on you. Go back to your support system. Trust your gut. Don't rush. Give yourself time to make the decision. Write out the different pros and cons of each decision. You likely already have the answer, you just aren't listening.

CHAPTER NINE

Don't Sell The Candy Store

> "Never give in. Never give in. Never, never, never, never - in nothing, great or small, large or petty - never give in, except to convictions of honor and good sense"
> **Winston Churchill**

I began to dread my time as a Carvel owner. But you wouldn't have thought that from the outside. I was making an above-average income when I was twenty-five to thirty years old, living the American dream: a beautiful home, great business, investment properties, frequent vacations, dream cars, etc... but I wasn't happy.

Every day was almost exactly the same, and it was kind of a no-brainer business after a while.

- Get to the store
- Put the ice cream in the machines
- Get everything cleaned up and ready to go
- Open the Carvel Store
- Customers come in
- Refill the ice cream machines
- Clean up the store for closing
- Take money to the bank
- Repeat again tomorrow

I remember one Saturday afternoon having to drive from Long Island to Brooklyn to pick up the money and I didn't even want to do that. It had gotten to the point where I felt my creative and mental energy was being zapped, and I wasn't being challenged enough mentally/intellectually. It was this inner turmoil because I was "living the dream," yet I didn't feel aligned anymore. I was so tired of driving on autopilot. Something was off.

What was I missing? I had the money and flexibility but still wasn't happy. I thought I was going crazy. How could I be unhappy when I had everything I wanted? Great wife, kids, family, three homes, thriving business, brand new cars, vacations, etc.

Flying from New York to Cabo, Mexico, Florida, and Texas. I was looking for the magic answer, stuck in a quagmire - "_How can I be this unhappy yet living this dream?_" It wasn't just about the time or money anymore.

Things had become stagnant in my career. The first year or two of owning the franchise was hard work, but after a while everything plateaued. I knew the business in and out. Nothing about it was challenging to me.

What I would have done differently...

Looking back now, I realize that I should have opened another Carvel franchise. I should have been running more than one, because it would have added more expertise and opportunity through branching out and having more staff under me. It was something I had thought about for some time, but I didn't pull the trigger and act on that thought.

After deciding to permanently close the failed convenience store, I lacked the confidence and was afraid to invest in something more costly. Despite having the money and the skill set to expand, fear ultimately held me back from a greater success. This was a point in my life where having a business mentor would have been a life-changer for me. Having someone with experience running multiple franchises would have helped me go to the next evolution of my career.

Instead, I decided to move to Arizona and sold my Carvel store in New York. Which turned out to be a catastrophe for me. I had my whole identity, my self-esteem, my whole life, wrapped up in that business.

It made me remember the Candy Store story I had heard long ago. In a lot of ways, I sold my candy store. Sure, I had my reasons for selling Carvel but looking back I could have made different decisions to slowly transition to my new life with my family in Arizona. My lack of planning and preparation led me to spiral into a really bad personal time.

I had no money coming in, and with my self-esteem, ego, and

essentially my entire identity being tied into how much money I made having a business, my emotional and mental well-being was not in a good place.

Nothing was working for me. I was maybe 30 or 31-years-old at this time. It got to the point where my wife and a few close friends had to have an intervention, if you will. They pulled me in and were like, "*Why don't you give up on your dream of being a business owner? It's obvious that this isn't working for you. You don't have any substantial income coming in to take care of your family. Why don't you just get a job?*"

But you've heard the rest of my story from this point. The mentorships I gained. The change in mindset I developed. The opportunities in unexpected places. There was something better on the horizon despite the storm I felt trapped in.

For a while I thought my "candy store" was Carvel, and in a lot of ways it was. But my story didn't end with me selling my Carvel franchise. It was just the beginning of my story as an entrepreneur. My business ventures didn't end with the selling of the physical store because the truth is that in my story, the candy store wasn't just some physical location.

The candy store in my story was the entrepreneurial spirit that I had within me from a young age. This spirit was there when I started working the newspaper route because of my desire to buy the things I wanted to buy with my own money. At a point when most kids were focused on simply having fun. I knew at a young age that the hard work would pay off.

During the turmoil of life stressors and financial struggles, I almost gave up on it. I had looked at giving up my dreams of working for myself - being self-employed and instead fitting myself into the mold of Corporate America. But I knew in my heart, and my gut, that it wasn't the right path for me. Which ultimately helped me find my way back to my candy store.

Choosing the path less traveled isn't always easy, but it is more than worth it. I can say that as someone who has spent the last 50 years experiencing it. Know that you aren't alone. You **can** achieve the success you want to experience in your life. Take one step at a time and before you know it, you'll be in awe of how far you've come.

***Don't give up on your dreams,
and don't sell the candy store.***

Growing up in Ridgewood, NY in 1950s. Friend Peter around 11

My father and I at Niagara Falls, 13 years old, around 1962

J3 Cub like the one I learned how to fly on, 1967

Basic Training in Fort Gordon, GA, 1968

Dating, 1972

My Carvel Franchise, 1973

Wedding Day, 1974

Parasailing during honeymoon, Acapulco, Mexico, 1974

Trip to Texas for Wedding, 1974

"The Babe" Cabin Cruiser 21', Brooklyn, 1976

Prompts

I don't want to leave you with my own lessons. I want to leave you with action steps as well. In this section you'll find several prompts. My suggestion would be to slowly work through each of these. If you've felt stuck, these should help you with finding redirection. I wish you the best on this journey called life. You've got this!

Where in your life could you use some thinking outside of the box?
_____
_____
_____
_____
_____
_____

Where are you struggling to get along with others?
_____
_____
_____
_____
_____
_____

Are you networking to build connections?
_____
_____
_____
_____
_____
_____

Who can you listen to who's further along the entrepreneurial path?
___

What would you do with financial freedom?
___

Are you sleeping too much?
___

What in your life is distracting you from your goals?
___

What are some good habits you can start creating in your life today?

_____
_____
_____
_____
_____
_____

What is a why big enough to keep you motivated on the hard days?

_____
_____
_____
_____
_____
_____

What vision do you have for your life?

_____
_____
_____
_____
_____
_____

How can you keep this vision front of mind when struggles arise? Because they will. It's not an if, but a when.

_____
_____
_____
_____
_____
_____

Who is in your corner? If you don't feel like you have anyone, how can you find those? Think about co-working opportunities, networking groups, etc.

_____
_____
_____
_____
_____
_____

In what ways are you allowing others to peer pressure you?

_____
_____
_____
_____
_____
_____

In what ways are your actions speaking louder than words? Remember Ralph Waldo Emerson's actions quote.

_____
_____
_____
_____
_____
_____

Are you working, honestly?

_____
_____
_____
_____
_____
_____

Are you being true to yourself?
___
___
___
___
___
___

Feeling stuck? What are options you might not have considered yet? Make a list of multiple different options. From silly to serious.
___
___
___
___
___
___

How are you letting your thoughts affect your successes?
___
___
___
___
___
___

How can you change your perspective on current situations?
___
___
___
___
___
___

Are you feeling sick about a situation you're in? Maybe a living situation or a career choice. Could it be your intuition/gut trying to tell you something?

_____
_____
_____
_____
_____
_____

If you could start all over, would you still do what you're doing now?

_____
_____
_____
_____
_____
_____

In what ways would you change if you knew you would succeed?

_____
_____
_____
_____
_____
_____

Are you afraid of success? A lot of people are and they self-sabotage.

_____
_____
_____
_____
_____
_____

What does your dream life look like?
_____
_____
_____
_____
_____
_____

Are you willing to pour into making your dream life come true?
_____
_____
_____
_____
_____
_____

Are you pushing past your comfort zone to achieve your goals? How?
_____
_____
_____
_____
_____
_____

Are you trying to sell your candy store? Why?
_____
_____
_____
_____
_____
_____

About The Author

Dennis Matzel has over 50 years of experience in business, management, and entrepreneurship. He owned and operated a high-volume Carvel Ice Cream Franchise at the age of 23. This venture opened the door to a lifetime of business ownership, consulting, investing, real estate portfolio management, and insurance brokerage. He partners with individuals, families, and businesses to help others reach their full potential and achieve successful financial outcomes.

After serving in the United States Army (including a tour in Vietnam), Dennis studied business, insurance, finance, and investment analysis, graduating from Brooklyn College, City University of New York (CUNY) with a B.A. in Economics.

Interested In Mentorship

Dennis O. Matzel
https://wisdomfinancialgrp.com
https://www.linkedin.com/in/dennis-matzel-86b2a11/
info@wisdomfinancialgrp.com

Wisdom Financial Group, LLC
8565 S. Eastern Ave #150
Las Vegas, NV 89123
(702) 336-4944

Rainy Day
SELF-PUBLISHING LLC

www.ingramcontent.com/pod-product-compliance
Lightning Source LLC
Chambersburg PA
CBHW060818050426
42449CB00008B/1718